50 Vegetarian Feast Recipes

By: Kelly Johnson

Table of Contents

- Roasted Vegetable Medley
- Eggplant Parmesan
- Spinach and Ricotta Stuffed Shells
- Vegetarian Chili
- Cauliflower Tacos
- Stuffed Bell Peppers
- Sweet Potato and Chickpea Curry
- Zucchini Noodles with Pesto
- Grilled Veggie Skewers
- Mushroom Risotto
- Spinach and Feta Quiche
- Veggie Burger Patties
- Baked Falafel with Hummus
- Butternut Squash Soup
- Veggie Sushi Rolls
- Caprese Salad with Balsamic Glaze
- Roasted Tomato and Garlic Pasta
- Tofu Stir-Fry with Vegetables
- Veggie Paella
- Stuffed Acorn Squash
- Vegetarian Lasagna
- Sweet Potato Fries
- Avocado and Tomato Salad
- Vegetable Samosas
- Greek Salad with Kalamata Olives
- Spaghetti Squash Primavera
- Roasted Carrot and Chickpea Salad
- Grilled Eggplant with Tahini Sauce
- Mushroom and Swiss Chard Pie
- Cabbage and Potato Pancakes
- Vegan Mushroom Wellington
- Broccoli and Cheese Stuffed Potatoes
- Lentil and Vegetable Shepherd's Pie
- Veggie and Hummus Wraps
- Cauliflower Fried Rice

- Tomato Basil Soup
- Falafel Salad with Tzatziki
- Spicy Roasted Cauliflower Tacos
- Chia Pudding with Berries
- Spinach and Artichoke Dip
- Grilled Portobello Mushroom Burgers
- Vegan Sloppy Joes
- Avocado Toast with Poached Egg
- Beetroot and Goat Cheese Salad
- Vegan Tacos with Guacamole
- Butternut Squash and Spinach Risotto
- Veggie Pot Pie
- Cauliflower Buffalo Wings
- Roasted Sweet Potato and Quinoa Salad
- Mushroom and Cheese Croquettes

Roasted Vegetable Medley

Ingredients:

- 2 cups cauliflower florets
- 1 cup broccoli florets
- 1 red bell pepper, sliced
- 1 zucchini, sliced
- 1 tbsp olive oil
- 1 tsp garlic powder
- 1/2 tsp paprika
- Salt and pepper to taste
- Fresh parsley, chopped (optional)

Instructions:

1. Preheat oven to 400°F (200°C).
2. Place cauliflower, broccoli, bell pepper, and zucchini on a baking sheet.
3. Drizzle with olive oil, then sprinkle garlic powder, paprika, salt, and pepper.
4. Toss the vegetables to coat evenly, then spread them in a single layer.
5. Roast for 20-25 minutes, or until tender and slightly browned, stirring halfway through.
6. Garnish with fresh parsley before serving.

Eggplant Parmesan

Ingredients:

- 2 large eggplants, sliced into 1/2-inch rounds
- 1 cup almond flour
- 2 large eggs, beaten
- 1 1/2 cups marinara sauce (sugar-free)
- 2 cups shredded mozzarella cheese
- 1/4 cup grated Parmesan cheese
- Olive oil for frying
- Salt and pepper to taste
- Fresh basil for garnish

Instructions:

1. Preheat oven to 375°F (190°C) and grease a baking dish.
2. Season eggplant slices with salt and pepper, then dip each slice into beaten eggs and coat with almond flour.
3. Heat olive oil in a skillet over medium heat. Fry eggplant slices for 2-3 minutes per side until golden.
4. Arrange fried eggplant slices in the baking dish, topping each with marinara sauce, mozzarella, and Parmesan.
5. Bake for 20-25 minutes until the cheese is melted and bubbly.
6. Garnish with fresh basil and serve hot.

Spinach and Ricotta Stuffed Shells

Ingredients:

- 12 large pasta shells, cooked
- 2 cups ricotta cheese
- 1 cup fresh spinach, chopped
- 1/2 cup grated Parmesan cheese
- 1 egg
- 2 cups marinara sauce
- 1 cup shredded mozzarella cheese
- Salt and pepper to taste

Instructions:

1. Preheat oven to 375°F (190°C).
2. In a bowl, mix ricotta, spinach, Parmesan, egg, salt, and pepper.
3. Stuff each pasta shell with the spinach and ricotta mixture.
4. Spread a thin layer of marinara sauce in a baking dish, then arrange the stuffed shells in the dish.
5. Top with the remaining marinara sauce and mozzarella cheese.
6. Bake for 20-25 minutes, or until the cheese is bubbly and golden.

Vegetarian Chili

Ingredients:

- 1 tbsp olive oil
- 1 onion, chopped
- 2 cloves garlic, minced
- 1 red bell pepper, chopped
- 1 zucchini, chopped
- 1 can (15 oz) black beans, drained and rinsed
- 1 can (15 oz) kidney beans, drained and rinsed
- 1 can (14.5 oz) diced tomatoes
- 1 cup vegetable broth
- 2 tbsp chili powder
- 1 tsp cumin
- 1/2 tsp paprika
- Salt and pepper to taste
- Fresh cilantro for garnish (optional)

Instructions:

1. Heat olive oil in a large pot over medium heat. Add onion and garlic, sautéing until softened.
2. Add bell pepper, zucchini, black beans, kidney beans, tomatoes, and vegetable broth.
3. Stir in chili powder, cumin, paprika, salt, and pepper.
4. Bring to a simmer and cook for 20-25 minutes, stirring occasionally.
5. Garnish with fresh cilantro and serve.

Cauliflower Tacos

Ingredients:

- 1 medium head of cauliflower, cut into florets
- 1 tbsp olive oil
- 1 tsp cumin
- 1 tsp chili powder
- Salt and pepper to taste
- Corn tortillas
- Toppings: avocado, salsa, shredded lettuce, cilantro, lime wedges

Instructions:

1. Preheat oven to 400°F (200°C).
2. Toss cauliflower florets with olive oil, cumin, chili powder, salt, and pepper.
3. Roast cauliflower on a baking sheet for 20-25 minutes, or until tender and slightly crispy.
4. Warm the tortillas in a dry skillet or microwave.
5. Assemble tacos by filling each tortilla with roasted cauliflower and your desired toppings.

Stuffed Bell Peppers

Ingredients:

- 4 bell peppers, tops cut off and seeds removed
- 1 cup cooked quinoa or rice
- 1 can (15 oz) black beans, drained and rinsed
- 1/2 cup corn kernels
- 1/2 cup shredded cheese (cheddar or Mexican blend)
- 1 tsp cumin
- 1 tsp chili powder
- Salt and pepper to taste
- 1/2 cup salsa

Instructions:

1. Preheat oven to 375°F (190°C).
2. In a bowl, mix quinoa or rice, black beans, corn, cheese, cumin, chili powder, salt, and pepper.
3. Stuff the bell peppers with the mixture and place them in a baking dish.
4. Pour salsa over the stuffed peppers and cover the dish with foil.
5. Bake for 25-30 minutes, removing the foil for the last 10 minutes to brown the tops.

Sweet Potato and Chickpea Curry

Ingredients:

- 1 tbsp olive oil
- 1 onion, chopped
- 2 cloves garlic, minced
- 1-inch piece of ginger, grated
- 1 large sweet potato, peeled and diced
- 1 can (15 oz) chickpeas, drained and rinsed
- 1 can (14 oz) coconut milk
- 1 can (14.5 oz) diced tomatoes
- 1 tbsp curry powder
- 1/2 tsp cumin
- Salt and pepper to taste
- Fresh cilantro for garnish

Instructions:

1. Heat olive oil in a large pot over medium heat. Add onion, garlic, and ginger, sautéing until softened.
2. Add sweet potato, chickpeas, coconut milk, diced tomatoes, curry powder, cumin, salt, and pepper.
3. Stir and bring to a simmer. Cook for 20-25 minutes, or until sweet potatoes are tender.
4. Garnish with fresh cilantro and serve.

Zucchini Noodles with Pesto

Ingredients:

- 2 large zucchinis, spiralized into noodles
- 1/2 cup fresh basil leaves
- 1/4 cup pine nuts
- 1/4 cup grated Parmesan cheese
- 1/4 cup olive oil
- 1 garlic clove
- Salt and pepper to taste

Instructions:

1. In a food processor, blend basil, pine nuts, Parmesan, olive oil, garlic, salt, and pepper until smooth.
2. Toss zucchini noodles with pesto sauce.
3. Serve immediately, garnished with extra Parmesan if desired.

Grilled Veggie Skewers

Ingredients:

- 1 zucchini, sliced into rounds
- 1 bell pepper, cut into chunks
- 1 red onion, cut into chunks
- 1 cup cherry tomatoes
- 1 tbsp olive oil
- 1 tsp Italian seasoning
- Salt and pepper to taste

Instructions:

1. Preheat grill to medium-high heat.
2. Thread zucchini, bell pepper, onion, and cherry tomatoes onto skewers.
3. Drizzle with olive oil and sprinkle with Italian seasoning, salt, and pepper.
4. Grill skewers for 8-10 minutes, turning occasionally, until vegetables are tender and lightly charred.
5. Serve hot.

Mushroom Risotto

Ingredients:

- 1 1/2 cups Arborio rice
- 2 tbsp olive oil
- 1 onion, finely chopped
- 2 cloves garlic, minced
- 4 cups vegetable broth
- 1 cup white wine (optional)
- 2 cups mushrooms, sliced
- 1/2 cup grated Parmesan cheese
- 2 tbsp butter
- Salt and pepper to taste
- Fresh parsley for garnish

Instructions:

1. Heat the vegetable broth in a saucepan and keep it warm on low heat.
2. In a large pan, heat olive oil over medium heat. Add the onion and garlic, sautéing until softened.
3. Add the mushrooms and cook until tender and browned.
4. Stir in the Arborio rice and cook for 2-3 minutes until lightly toasted.
5. Pour in the white wine (if using) and stir until absorbed.
6. Gradually add the warm vegetable broth, one ladleful at a time, stirring constantly. Wait until the liquid is absorbed before adding more broth.
7. Continue until the rice is creamy and tender (about 20-25 minutes).
8. Stir in the Parmesan cheese, butter, salt, and pepper.
9. Garnish with fresh parsley and serve.

Spinach and Feta Quiche

Ingredients:

- 1 pre-made pie crust
- 2 cups fresh spinach, chopped
- 1 cup feta cheese, crumbled
- 4 large eggs
- 1 cup milk or heavy cream
- 1/2 tsp nutmeg
- Salt and pepper to taste
- 1 tbsp olive oil

Instructions:

1. Preheat oven to 375°F (190°C).
2. Heat olive oil in a pan over medium heat. Add spinach and cook until wilted, about 2-3 minutes.
3. In a bowl, whisk together eggs, milk, nutmeg, salt, and pepper.
4. Spread the cooked spinach evenly in the pie crust and sprinkle with feta cheese.
5. Pour the egg mixture over the spinach and cheese.
6. Bake for 35-40 minutes, or until the quiche is set and lightly golden.
7. Let cool slightly before slicing and serving.

Veggie Burger Patties

Ingredients:

- 1 cup cooked quinoa
- 1 cup cooked black beans, mashed
- 1/2 cup breadcrumbs
- 1/2 cup grated carrot
- 1/4 cup chopped onion
- 2 cloves garlic, minced
- 1 tsp cumin
- 1/2 tsp paprika
- Salt and pepper to taste
- 1 tbsp olive oil

Instructions:

1. In a bowl, combine quinoa, black beans, breadcrumbs, carrot, onion, garlic, cumin, paprika, salt, and pepper.
2. Mix everything until well combined. Shape into patties.
3. Heat olive oil in a skillet over medium heat. Cook patties for 3-4 minutes per side, until golden brown.
4. Serve on buns with your favorite toppings.

Baked Falafel with Hummus

Ingredients:

- 1 can (15 oz) chickpeas, drained and rinsed
- 1/2 cup chopped onion
- 2 cloves garlic, minced
- 1/4 cup fresh parsley
- 1 tsp cumin
- 1 tsp coriander
- 2 tbsp flour
- Salt and pepper to taste
- Olive oil for drizzling
- Hummus for serving

Instructions:

1. Preheat oven to 375°F (190°C).
2. In a food processor, combine chickpeas, onion, garlic, parsley, cumin, coriander, flour, salt, and pepper. Pulse until smooth but slightly chunky.
3. Shape the mixture into small balls or patties and place them on a baking sheet.
4. Drizzle with olive oil and bake for 20-25 minutes, turning halfway, until golden brown.
5. Serve with hummus.

Butternut Squash Soup

Ingredients:

- 1 medium butternut squash, peeled and diced
- 1 onion, chopped
- 2 cloves garlic, minced
- 4 cups vegetable broth
- 1/2 tsp cinnamon
- 1/4 tsp nutmeg
- Salt and pepper to taste
- 2 tbsp olive oil
- 1/2 cup coconut milk (optional)

Instructions:

1. Preheat oven to 400°F (200°C). Spread the butternut squash on a baking sheet, drizzle with olive oil, and roast for 25-30 minutes, until tender.
2. In a large pot, sauté onion and garlic in olive oil over medium heat until softened.
3. Add the roasted butternut squash, vegetable broth, cinnamon, nutmeg, salt, and pepper. Bring to a simmer.
4. Blend the soup until smooth using an immersion blender or regular blender.
5. Stir in coconut milk, if using, and adjust seasoning.
6. Serve hot.

Veggie Sushi Rolls

Ingredients:

- 2 cups sushi rice, cooked
- 1 sheet nori (seaweed)
- 1/2 cucumber, julienned
- 1/2 avocado, sliced
- 1/2 carrot, julienned
- 1/4 cup rice vinegar
- 1 tsp sugar
- Soy sauce for dipping

Instructions:

1. Mix rice vinegar and sugar in a bowl until the sugar dissolves. Gently fold the mixture into the cooked sushi rice.
2. Place a sheet of nori on a bamboo sushi mat, shiny side down.
3. Spread a thin layer of rice on the nori, leaving about 1 inch at the top free.
4. Arrange cucumber, avocado, and carrot along the bottom edge of the rice.
5. Roll the sushi tightly, using the mat to help shape it.
6. Slice the roll into 6-8 pieces and serve with soy sauce.

Caprese Salad with Balsamic Glaze

Ingredients:

- 2 large tomatoes, sliced
- 1 ball fresh mozzarella, sliced
- Fresh basil leaves
- Salt and pepper to taste
- Balsamic glaze for drizzling

Instructions:

1. Arrange tomato slices, mozzarella slices, and basil leaves on a plate.
2. Drizzle with balsamic glaze and season with salt and pepper.
3. Serve immediately.

Roasted Tomato and Garlic Pasta

Ingredients:

- 2 cups cherry tomatoes, halved
- 3 cloves garlic, minced
- 2 tbsp olive oil
- 1 lb pasta of choice
- 1/4 cup fresh basil, chopped
- Salt and pepper to taste
- Grated Parmesan for serving

Instructions:

1. Preheat oven to 400°F (200°C). Toss tomatoes and garlic with olive oil, salt, and pepper. Roast for 15-20 minutes.
2. Cook pasta according to package instructions.
3. Toss cooked pasta with roasted tomatoes, garlic, and fresh basil.
4. Serve with grated Parmesan.

Tofu Stir-Fry with Vegetables

Ingredients:

- 1 block firm tofu, pressed and cubed
- 1 cup bell peppers, sliced
- 1/2 cup broccoli florets
- 1/2 cup carrots, julienned
- 2 tbsp soy sauce
- 1 tbsp sesame oil
- 1 tbsp rice vinegar
- 1 tbsp honey or maple syrup
- 1 tsp ginger, grated
- 1 tsp garlic, minced
- Sesame seeds for garnish

Instructions:

1. In a pan, sauté tofu in sesame oil until golden brown. Remove and set aside.
2. In the same pan, sauté garlic and ginger until fragrant. Add the vegetables and cook until tender.
3. Stir in soy sauce, rice vinegar, and honey.
4. Add tofu back into the pan and toss to combine.
5. Garnish with sesame seeds and serve.

Veggie Paella

Ingredients:

- 1 tbsp olive oil
- 1 onion, chopped
- 1 bell pepper, chopped
- 2 tomatoes, chopped
- 1 1/2 cups Arborio rice
- 3 cups vegetable broth
- 1/2 cup peas
- 1/2 cup artichoke hearts, chopped
- 1 tsp paprika
- 1/2 tsp saffron (optional)
- Salt and pepper to taste

Instructions:

1. Heat olive oil in a large pan. Sauté onion, bell pepper, and tomatoes until softened.
2. Add the rice, vegetable broth, peas, artichoke hearts, paprika, saffron, salt, and pepper.
3. Bring to a boil, then reduce heat and simmer, covered, for 20-25 minutes, until the rice is tender.
4. Let rest for 5 minutes before serving.

Stuffed Acorn Squash

Ingredients:

- 2 acorn squash, halved and seeds removed
- 1 cup cooked quinoa
- 1/2 cup cranberries (dried or fresh)
- 1/4 cup walnuts, chopped
- 1/4 cup feta cheese, crumbled
- 1 tbsp olive oil
- 1 tsp cinnamon
- Salt and pepper to taste
- Fresh parsley for garnish

Instructions:

1. Preheat oven to 375°F (190°C).
2. Place acorn squash halves on a baking sheet and drizzle with olive oil. Season with salt, pepper, and cinnamon.
3. Roast squash for 40-45 minutes, until tender.
4. In a bowl, mix quinoa, cranberries, walnuts, and feta.
5. Once the squash is done, stuff it with the quinoa mixture.
6. Garnish with fresh parsley and serve.

Vegetarian Lasagna

Ingredients:

- 9 lasagna noodles, cooked
- 1 jar marinara sauce
- 1/2 cup ricotta cheese
- 2 cups shredded mozzarella cheese
- 1 cup spinach, chopped
- 1 zucchini, sliced
- 1/2 cup mushrooms, sliced
- 1 tbsp olive oil
- 1 tsp dried oregano
- Salt and pepper to taste

Instructions:

1. Preheat oven to 375°F (190°C).
2. Heat olive oil in a pan and sauté zucchini, mushrooms, and spinach until soft.
3. Spread a layer of marinara sauce in the bottom of a baking dish.
4. Place a layer of lasagna noodles on top, followed by ricotta cheese, sautéed vegetables, marinara sauce, and mozzarella.
5. Repeat the layers, finishing with mozzarella on top.
6. Bake for 30-35 minutes, until bubbly and golden.
7. Let cool for a few minutes before slicing and serving.

Sweet Potato Fries

Ingredients:

- 2 large sweet potatoes, peeled and cut into fries
- 2 tbsp olive oil
- 1 tsp paprika
- 1/2 tsp garlic powder
- Salt and pepper to taste

Instructions:

1. Preheat oven to 425°F (220°C).
2. Toss sweet potato fries in olive oil, paprika, garlic powder, salt, and pepper.
3. Spread fries in a single layer on a baking sheet.
4. Bake for 25-30 minutes, flipping halfway through, until crispy.
5. Serve immediately.

Avocado and Tomato Salad

Ingredients:

- 2 ripe avocados, diced
- 2 large tomatoes, diced
- 1/4 red onion, thinly sliced
- 1 tbsp olive oil
- 1 tbsp fresh lime juice
- Salt and pepper to taste
- Fresh cilantro for garnish

Instructions:

1. In a bowl, combine avocados, tomatoes, and red onion.
2. Drizzle with olive oil and lime juice. Toss gently to combine.
3. Season with salt and pepper.
4. Garnish with fresh cilantro and serve immediately.

Vegetable Samosas

Ingredients:

- 1 cup mixed vegetables (peas, carrots, potatoes), cooked and mashed
- 1/2 onion, finely chopped
- 1 tsp cumin
- 1 tsp coriander
- 1/2 tsp turmeric
- 1/2 tsp garam masala
- 1 tbsp olive oil
- 8-10 samosa wrappers (or phyllo dough)
- Salt and pepper to taste
- Oil for frying

Instructions:

1. Heat olive oil in a pan and sauté onions until soft.
2. Add spices and cook for 1-2 minutes, until fragrant.
3. Stir in mashed vegetables, salt, and pepper. Cook for another 5 minutes.
4. Let the filling cool slightly.
5. Fill samosa wrappers with the vegetable mixture, folding into triangles and sealing edges with water.
6. Heat oil in a pan and fry samosas until golden and crispy, about 3-4 minutes.
7. Serve with chutney.

Greek Salad with Kalamata Olives

Ingredients:

- 2 cups cucumber, diced
- 1 cup cherry tomatoes, halved
- 1/2 red onion, thinly sliced
- 1 cup Kalamata olives
- 1/2 cup feta cheese, crumbled
- 2 tbsp olive oil
- 1 tbsp red wine vinegar
- 1 tsp dried oregano
- Salt and pepper to taste

Instructions:

1. In a bowl, combine cucumber, tomatoes, onion, olives, and feta.
2. Drizzle with olive oil and red wine vinegar.
3. Sprinkle with oregano, salt, and pepper.
4. Toss gently and serve.

Spaghetti Squash Primavera

Ingredients:

- 1 medium spaghetti squash, halved and seeds removed
- 2 tbsp olive oil
- 1 bell pepper, sliced
- 1 zucchini, sliced
- 1 cup cherry tomatoes, halved
- 2 cloves garlic, minced
- 1/4 cup Parmesan cheese, grated
- Salt and pepper to taste
- Fresh basil for garnish

Instructions:

1. Preheat oven to 400°F (200°C). Place spaghetti squash halves on a baking sheet, drizzle with olive oil, and season with salt and pepper.
2. Roast for 40-45 minutes, until tender.
3. While squash is roasting, heat olive oil in a pan and sauté bell pepper, zucchini, and tomatoes until soft.
4. Scrape the roasted squash with a fork to create spaghetti-like strands.
5. Toss the squash with sautéed vegetables, garlic, and Parmesan.
6. Garnish with fresh basil and serve.

Roasted Carrot and Chickpea Salad

Ingredients:

- 4 large carrots, peeled and sliced
- 1 can (15 oz) chickpeas, drained and rinsed
- 2 tbsp olive oil
- 1 tsp cumin
- 1/2 tsp paprika
- Salt and pepper to taste
- Fresh parsley for garnish
- 1 tbsp tahini (optional)

Instructions:

1. Preheat oven to 400°F (200°C).
2. Toss carrots and chickpeas in olive oil, cumin, paprika, salt, and pepper.
3. Spread on a baking sheet and roast for 25-30 minutes, until carrots are tender.
4. Drizzle with tahini, if desired, and garnish with fresh parsley.
5. Serve warm or at room temperature.

Grilled Eggplant with Tahini Sauce

Ingredients:

- 2 eggplants, sliced into rounds
- 2 tbsp olive oil
- Salt and pepper to taste
- 1/4 cup tahini
- 1 tbsp lemon juice
- 1 tbsp water (adjust for consistency)
- 1 clove garlic, minced
- Fresh parsley for garnish

Instructions:

1. Preheat grill or grill pan over medium heat.
2. Brush eggplant slices with olive oil and season with salt and pepper.
3. Grill eggplant slices for 4-5 minutes per side, until tender and charred.
4. In a bowl, whisk together tahini, lemon juice, water, garlic, salt, and pepper to make the sauce.
5. Drizzle the tahini sauce over the grilled eggplant slices.
6. Garnish with fresh parsley and serve.

Mushroom and Swiss Chard Pie

Ingredients:

- 1 sheet of puff pastry (store-bought or homemade)
- 2 tbsp olive oil
- 2 cups mushrooms, sliced
- 1 bunch Swiss chard, chopped
- 1/2 onion, finely chopped
- 2 cloves garlic, minced
- 1/4 cup vegetable broth
- 1/2 tsp thyme
- 1/4 tsp nutmeg
- Salt and pepper to taste
- 1/4 cup heavy cream or dairy-free cream
- 1 egg (for egg wash, optional)

Instructions:

1. Preheat oven to 375°F (190°C).
2. In a pan, heat olive oil over medium heat and sauté onions and garlic until soft.
3. Add mushrooms and Swiss chard, cooking until the mushrooms release moisture and the chard wilts.
4. Stir in vegetable broth, thyme, nutmeg, salt, and pepper. Cook for 5 minutes until the mixture thickens.
5. Remove from heat and stir in heavy cream.
6. Roll out the puff pastry on a baking sheet. Spoon the mushroom mixture into the center and fold the edges of the pastry over the filling.
7. If using, brush with a beaten egg for a golden finish.
8. Bake for 25-30 minutes, or until the pastry is golden and flaky. Let cool slightly before serving.

Cabbage and Potato Pancakes

Ingredients:

- 2 medium potatoes, peeled and grated
- 1/2 small cabbage, shredded
- 1/4 onion, grated
- 1 egg, beaten
- 2 tbsp flour (gluten-free or regular)
- 1/2 tsp salt
- 1/4 tsp black pepper
- 1/4 tsp paprika
- Olive oil for frying

Instructions:

1. Place grated potatoes in a clean kitchen towel and squeeze out excess moisture.
2. In a large bowl, mix grated potatoes, cabbage, onion, egg, flour, salt, pepper, and paprika until well combined.
3. Heat olive oil in a skillet over medium heat.
4. Scoop spoonfuls of the mixture into the pan and flatten them into pancakes. Cook for 3-4 minutes per side, until golden brown and crispy.
5. Serve hot with sour cream or apple sauce.

Vegan Mushroom Wellington

Ingredients:

- 1 sheet puff pastry (vegan)
- 2 cups mushrooms, chopped
- 1 tbsp olive oil
- 1/2 onion, chopped
- 2 cloves garlic, minced
- 1/4 cup fresh parsley, chopped
- 1/2 cup spinach, chopped
- 1 tbsp soy sauce
- 1 tsp thyme
- 1/4 cup breadcrumbs (optional)
- Salt and pepper to taste
- 1 tbsp olive oil for brushing

Instructions:

1. Preheat oven to 400°F (200°C).
2. Heat olive oil in a pan over medium heat, and sauté onions and garlic until softened.
3. Add mushrooms and cook until they release moisture and reduce, about 5-7 minutes.
4. Stir in soy sauce, thyme, parsley, spinach, salt, and pepper. Cook until spinach wilts and moisture evaporates.
5. Roll out puff pastry on a baking sheet. Place the mushroom mixture in the center, and fold the pastry over to seal.
6. Brush with olive oil, then bake for 25-30 minutes, until golden and crispy.
7. Let cool for 10 minutes before slicing.

Broccoli and Cheese Stuffed Potatoes

Ingredients:

- 4 medium potatoes
- 1 cup broccoli florets, steamed
- 1/2 cup shredded cheddar cheese (or dairy-free cheese)
- 2 tbsp sour cream or vegan sour cream
- 2 tbsp butter or olive oil
- Salt and pepper to taste

Instructions:

1. Preheat oven to 400°F (200°C).
2. Pierce potatoes with a fork and bake directly on the oven rack for 40-45 minutes, until tender.
3. While potatoes bake, steam broccoli until tender, then chop finely.
4. Once potatoes are baked, slice them open and scoop out the flesh, leaving a thin border around the edges.
5. Mash the potato flesh with sour cream, butter, salt, and pepper. Stir in steamed broccoli and cheese.
6. Stuff the mashed mixture back into the potato skins, then return them to the oven for 10 minutes.
7. Serve warm.

Lentil and Vegetable Shepherd's Pie

Ingredients:

- 1 cup lentils, cooked
- 1/2 cup carrots, diced
- 1/2 cup peas
- 1 onion, chopped
- 2 cloves garlic, minced
- 2 tbsp tomato paste
- 2 cups vegetable broth
- 1/4 tsp thyme
- Salt and pepper to taste
- 3 large potatoes, peeled and mashed
- 1/4 cup vegan butter or regular butter

Instructions:

1. Preheat oven to 375°F (190°C).
2. In a large pan, sauté onion, garlic, and carrots in olive oil until softened.
3. Add garlic and cook for another minute. Stir in lentils, peas, tomato paste, vegetable broth, thyme, salt, and pepper. Let simmer for 10-15 minutes until thickened.
4. Transfer the lentil mixture to a baking dish, spreading it evenly.
5. Top with mashed potatoes and smooth the top.
6. Bake for 20-25 minutes until golden on top. Serve hot.

Veggie and Hummus Wraps

Ingredients:

- 4 whole wheat wraps
- 1/2 cup hummus
- 1 cucumber, sliced
- 1 avocado, sliced
- 1/2 red pepper, sliced
- 1/2 carrot, grated
- 1 cup mixed greens
- Salt and pepper to taste

Instructions:

1. Lay out the wraps and spread a generous layer of hummus on each.
2. Top with cucumber, avocado, red pepper, carrot, and mixed greens.
3. Season with salt and pepper.
4. Roll the wraps tightly and slice in half. Serve immediately.

Cauliflower Fried Rice

Ingredients:

- 1 small head cauliflower, grated into rice-sized pieces
- 2 tbsp olive oil
- 1/2 onion, chopped
- 2 cloves garlic, minced
- 1/2 cup frozen peas and carrots
- 2 eggs, beaten (or tofu for vegan option)
- 3 tbsp soy sauce
- Salt and pepper to taste
- Green onions for garnish

Instructions:

1. Heat olive oil in a large pan and sauté onions and garlic until softened.
2. Add peas and carrots, and cook for 2-3 minutes.
3. Push the veggies to the side and scramble the eggs in the pan, then combine with the veggies.
4. Add cauliflower rice and soy sauce, cooking for 5-7 minutes until tender.
5. Season with salt and pepper and garnish with green onions.

Tomato Basil Soup

Ingredients:

- 6 ripe tomatoes, chopped
- 1 onion, chopped
- 2 cloves garlic, minced
- 2 cups vegetable broth
- 1 tsp dried basil
- Salt and pepper to taste
- 1/4 cup fresh basil, chopped
- 1 tbsp olive oil

Instructions:

1. Heat olive oil in a large pot and sauté onions and garlic until softened.
2. Add chopped tomatoes, vegetable broth, dried basil, salt, and pepper. Simmer for 15-20 minutes.
3. Use an immersion blender or regular blender to puree the soup until smooth.
4. Stir in fresh basil and serve warm.

Falafel Salad with Tzatziki

Ingredients:

- 1 can chickpeas, drained and mashed
- 1/2 onion, finely chopped
- 2 cloves garlic, minced
- 1 tbsp cumin
- 1 tbsp coriander
- 2 tbsp fresh parsley, chopped
- 1/4 cup flour
- Salt and pepper to taste
- 1 tbsp olive oil for frying
- Mixed greens for the salad
- 1/2 cucumber, sliced
- Cherry tomatoes for garnish

For Tzatziki:

- 1 cup Greek yogurt
- 1/2 cucumber, grated
- 1 clove garlic, minced
- 1 tbsp olive oil
- 1 tbsp lemon juice
- Salt and pepper to taste

Instructions:

1. In a bowl, combine mashed chickpeas, onion, garlic, spices, parsley, flour, salt, and pepper. Form into small balls.
2. Heat olive oil in a pan and fry falafel balls until golden brown on all sides.
3. Mix tzatziki ingredients together in a bowl and season with salt and pepper.
4. Serve falafel over mixed greens, cucumber, and cherry tomatoes with a generous drizzle of tzatziki.

Spicy Roasted Cauliflower Tacos

Ingredients:

- 1 medium cauliflower, cut into florets
- 2 tbsp olive oil
- 1 tsp chili powder
- 1/2 tsp cumin
- 1/4 tsp smoked paprika
- Salt and pepper to taste
- 8 small tortillas
- 1/2 cup cilantro, chopped
- 1/2 red onion, thinly sliced
- Lime wedges for serving

Instructions:

1. Preheat oven to 400°F (200°C).
2. Toss cauliflower with olive oil, chili powder, cumin, paprika, salt, and pepper.
3. Spread on a baking sheet and roast for 20-25 minutes, flipping halfway through, until tender and crispy.
4. Warm tortillas and fill with roasted cauliflower, cilantro, and red onion.
5. Serve with lime wedges.

Chia Pudding with Berries

Ingredients:

- 1/4 cup chia seeds
- 1 cup almond milk (or any plant-based milk)
- 1 tsp vanilla extract
- 1 tbsp maple syrup or honey (optional)
- 1/2 cup mixed berries (blueberries, raspberries, strawberries)
- Fresh mint for garnish (optional)

Instructions:

1. In a bowl, combine chia seeds, almond milk, vanilla extract, and maple syrup. Stir well to combine.
2. Let the mixture sit for 10 minutes and then stir again to ensure the chia seeds are evenly distributed.
3. Cover and refrigerate for at least 2 hours or overnight until it thickens to a pudding-like consistency.
4. Top with mixed berries and garnish with fresh mint before serving.

Spinach and Artichoke Dip

Ingredients:

- 1 can artichoke hearts, drained and chopped
- 2 cups fresh spinach, chopped
- 1/2 cup cream cheese (or vegan cream cheese)
- 1/2 cup Greek yogurt (or dairy-free yogurt)
- 1/2 cup Parmesan cheese (or nutritional yeast for vegan)
- 1/4 cup garlic, minced
- 1 tbsp olive oil
- Salt and pepper to taste

Instructions:

1. Preheat the oven to 375°F (190°C).
2. In a pan, heat olive oil and sauté garlic until fragrant.
3. Add chopped spinach and cook until wilted, about 3-4 minutes.
4. In a mixing bowl, combine cream cheese, yogurt, Parmesan, artichokes, spinach, salt, and pepper. Stir until smooth.
5. Transfer the mixture to a baking dish and bake for 20-25 minutes, or until golden and bubbly.
6. Serve with tortilla chips, crackers, or vegetable sticks.

Grilled Portobello Mushroom Burgers

Ingredients:

- 4 large Portobello mushroom caps
- 2 tbsp balsamic vinegar
- 2 tbsp olive oil
- 1 tsp garlic powder
- 1 tsp dried thyme
- Salt and pepper to taste
- 4 whole wheat buns or burger buns of choice
- Lettuce, tomato, onion, and other toppings (optional)

Instructions:

1. Preheat the grill or grill pan to medium-high heat.
2. In a small bowl, mix olive oil, balsamic vinegar, garlic powder, thyme, salt, and pepper.
3. Brush the mushroom caps with the marinade on both sides.
4. Grill the mushrooms for 5-7 minutes per side, until tender and juicy.
5. Toast the buns on the grill for 1-2 minutes.
6. Assemble the burgers by placing the grilled mushrooms on the buns and adding your favorite toppings. Serve hot.

Vegan Sloppy Joes

Ingredients:

- 1 can lentils, drained and rinsed
- 1 onion, chopped
- 1 bell pepper, chopped
- 2 cloves garlic, minced
- 1 cup tomato sauce
- 2 tbsp tomato paste
- 1 tbsp soy sauce or tamari
- 1 tbsp maple syrup
- 1 tsp smoked paprika
- 1/2 tsp chili powder
- 1/4 tsp cumin
- Salt and pepper to taste
- 4 whole wheat buns

Instructions:

1. In a large pan, heat oil and sauté onions, bell pepper, and garlic until soft.
2. Add the lentils, tomato sauce, tomato paste, soy sauce, maple syrup, paprika, chili powder, cumin, salt, and pepper. Stir to combine.
3. Simmer for 10-15 minutes, until the mixture thickens.
4. Toast the buns and scoop the lentil mixture onto the bottom half of each bun.
5. Top with the other half of the bun and serve.

Avocado Toast with Poached Egg

Ingredients:

- 2 slices of whole wheat bread or your favorite bread
- 1 ripe avocado
- 2 eggs
- 1 tsp white vinegar
- Salt and pepper to taste
- Red pepper flakes or lemon juice for garnish (optional)

Instructions:

1. Toast the bread slices until crispy.
2. In a small pot, bring water to a simmer, add vinegar, and gently add the eggs one at a time. Cook for 3-4 minutes until the whites are set but the yolk is runny.
3. While the eggs cook, mash the avocado with a fork and season with salt and pepper.
4. Spread the mashed avocado onto the toasted bread.
5. Gently place the poached eggs on top, garnish with red pepper flakes or lemon juice if desired, and serve.

Beetroot and Goat Cheese Salad

Ingredients:

- 2 medium beets, roasted and sliced
- 1/4 cup goat cheese, crumbled
- 2 cups mixed greens (arugula, spinach, or lettuce)
- 1/4 cup walnuts, toasted
- 1/2 small red onion, thinly sliced
- 1 tbsp balsamic vinegar
- 1 tbsp olive oil
- Salt and pepper to taste

Instructions:

1. Preheat the oven to 400°F (200°C). Wrap beets in foil and roast for 40-45 minutes, until tender. Peel and slice once cooled.
2. In a large bowl, combine mixed greens, beets, goat cheese, walnuts, and red onion.
3. Drizzle with balsamic vinegar and olive oil, and season with salt and pepper.
4. Toss to combine and serve.

Vegan Tacos with Guacamole

Ingredients:

- 1 can black beans, drained and rinsed
- 1 tsp cumin
- 1/2 tsp chili powder
- Salt and pepper to taste
- 8 small corn tortillas
- 1 avocado
- 1 tbsp lime juice
- 1/4 cup red onion, diced
- 1/4 cup cilantro, chopped
- 1/2 cup lettuce, shredded
- Salsa and hot sauce for garnish (optional)

Instructions:

1. In a pan, heat the black beans with cumin, chili powder, salt, and pepper. Cook for 5-7 minutes, mashing slightly with a fork.
2. In a bowl, mash the avocado with lime juice, red onion, and cilantro to make the guacamole.
3. Warm the tortillas in a dry pan or microwave.
4. Assemble the tacos by filling each tortilla with black beans, guacamole, lettuce, and salsa or hot sauce.
5. Serve immediately.

Butternut Squash and Spinach Risotto

Ingredients:

- 1 cup Arborio rice
- 1 small butternut squash, peeled and diced
- 2 cups fresh spinach, chopped
- 1/2 onion, chopped
- 2 cloves garlic, minced
- 4 cups vegetable broth
- 1/2 cup white wine (optional)
- 2 tbsp olive oil
- 1/4 cup Parmesan cheese (or nutritional yeast for vegan)
- Salt and pepper to taste

Instructions:

1. Preheat the oven to 400°F (200°C). Toss butternut squash with olive oil, salt, and pepper, then roast for 20-25 minutes, or until tender.
2. In a large pan, heat olive oil and sauté onion and garlic until soft.
3. Add the rice and cook for 1-2 minutes, stirring constantly. Add the white wine (if using) and cook until absorbed.
4. Gradually add the vegetable broth, one ladle at a time, stirring constantly and allowing each addition to be absorbed before adding more.
5. When the rice is creamy and tender (about 18-20 minutes), stir in the roasted butternut squash and spinach.
6. Add Parmesan cheese (or nutritional yeast) and adjust seasoning with salt and pepper.
7. Serve warm.

Veggie Pot Pie

Ingredients:

- 1 sheet puff pastry or pie crust
- 2 cups mixed vegetables (carrots, peas, corn, green beans)
- 1/2 cup onion, chopped
- 2 cloves garlic, minced
- 1/4 cup flour
- 2 cups vegetable broth
- 1/2 cup plant-based milk (or regular milk)
- 1 tbsp olive oil
- 1 tsp thyme
- Salt and pepper to taste

Instructions:

1. Preheat the oven to 375°F (190°C). Roll out the puff pastry to fit a pie dish.
2. In a large pan, heat olive oil and sauté onion and garlic until softened.
3. Add the mixed vegetables and cook for 5-7 minutes.
4. Sprinkle flour over the vegetables and stir to coat. Gradually add vegetable broth and plant-based milk, stirring continuously until thickened.
5. Stir in thyme, salt, and pepper.
6. Pour the vegetable mixture into the prepared pie dish and top with the puff pastry. Trim any excess pastry and crimp the edges.
7. Bake for 30-35 minutes, or until the crust is golden brown. Let cool for a few minutes before serving.

Cauliflower Buffalo Wings

Ingredients:

- 1 head of cauliflower, cut into florets
- 1 cup flour
- 1/2 cup water
- 1 tsp garlic powder
- 1 tsp onion powder
- 1/2 tsp paprika
- Salt and pepper to taste
- 1 cup buffalo sauce
- 2 tbsp olive oil

Instructions:

1. Preheat the oven to 400°F (200°C). Line a baking sheet with parchment paper.
2. In a large bowl, mix flour, water, garlic powder, onion powder, paprika, salt, and pepper to create a batter.
3. Dip each cauliflower floret into the batter, coating evenly, and place them on the prepared baking sheet.
4. Bake for 20-25 minutes, flipping halfway through, until golden and crispy.
5. In a separate bowl, toss the baked cauliflower wings with buffalo sauce.
6. Serve with celery and ranch or blue cheese dressing (optional).

Roasted Sweet Potato and Quinoa Salad

Ingredients:

- 2 medium sweet potatoes, peeled and cubed
- 1 cup quinoa, cooked
- 1/2 cup red onion, diced
- 1/4 cup cranberries (optional)
- 1/4 cup chopped parsley
- 1 tbsp olive oil
- 1 tbsp balsamic vinegar
- Salt and pepper to taste

Instructions:

1. Preheat the oven to 400°F (200°C). Toss sweet potato cubes with olive oil, salt, and pepper, and roast for 25-30 minutes, or until tender.
2. Cook quinoa according to package instructions.
3. In a large bowl, combine roasted sweet potatoes, quinoa, red onion, cranberries, and parsley.
4. Drizzle with balsamic vinegar, toss gently, and season with salt and pepper.
5. Serve warm or at room temperature.

Mushroom and Cheese Croquettes

Ingredients:

- 2 cups mushrooms, finely chopped
- 1/2 cup grated cheese (cheddar, mozzarella, or your choice)
- 1/4 cup breadcrumbs (or gluten-free breadcrumbs)
- 2 tbsp flour (or gluten-free flour)
- 2 tbsp plant-based milk (or regular milk)
- 1 egg (or flax egg for vegan)
- Salt and pepper to taste
- Olive oil for frying

Instructions:

1. In a pan, heat olive oil and sauté chopped mushrooms until soft and the moisture has evaporated, about 5-7 minutes.
2. In a bowl, combine the cooked mushrooms, grated cheese, breadcrumbs, flour, and plant-based milk. Add salt and pepper to taste.
3. Shape the mixture into small croquettes or balls.
4. Dip each croquette into the egg (or flax egg), then coat in additional breadcrumbs.
5. Heat olive oil in a pan and fry the croquettes for 3-4 minutes per side, or until golden brown.
6. Drain on paper towels and serve warm with your favorite dipping sauce.